Dead Men's S

Contents

1

Tom and Reg

Tom went to join the queue of men

waiting for the van to arrive.

There was no sign of Reg.

He would miss a free meal

if he didn't come soon.

Tom pushed his way to the front.

It didn't do to be too polite

in an area where there were lots

of people living on the streets.

A buzz went up from the crowd
as the van came into sight.
It drew up and a girl got out.
It was the pretty one, Gina, today.
The driver, a young man called Des,
came round to help her open the doors.
'Steady on, gents,' he said.
'One at a time please.'

He and Gina began to hand out the food.
The sandwiches, pies and sausage rolls
that they collected every night
from the big stores after closing time.
Food that would have been thrown away
because it was past its sell-by date.
Tom held out his hand
for a packet of sandwiches.
He asked for some for Reg.
'My friend's late,' he said.

'Sorry,' Des told him.

'You know the rules.

Only one item per person.'

Gina tapped him on the arm.

She pointed to Reg
making his way down the street.
'His mate's coming now.
Let him have it.'
She smiled at Tom.
'OK love?' she said.

Reg came up puffing and panting.
'Slow down,' Tom told him.
'I got you a pie. Want to share?'
The two men went to a quiet spot.
Away from the troublemakers
who'd snatch the food from them.
Away from the drunks and the young kids
out of their heads on drugs.
Tom hated to see them. It upset him.
'What a waste,' he said.
'We're old. They've got their
whole lives ahead of them.'

Tom split open the pack of sandwiches.

He gave one to Reg.

'Cheese again,' he said.

Reg broke his pie in two,

handed half to Tom.

They began to eat, saying nothing.

Afterwards Tom licked his fingers.

He dabbed at the crumbs on his coat

and sucked them into his mouth.

Reg pulled a face.

Even though he was down and out

he cared about good manners.

He had been quite well off once

and he never let Tom forget it.

He didn't like the charity workers.

'Do-gooders, the lot of them,' he said.

'He still eats the pies though,'

Tom thought.

2

The Shoes

Tom took some stub ends from his pocket.

He pulled the strands of tobacco out.

'Fancy a roll up?' he asked.

Reg shook his head.

'The nights are getting cold,' he said.

'Yes.' Tom dreaded the winter coming.

His boots had holes in them.

His feet got wet

every time it rained.

'I hear that STREET AID lot are coming round,
this week,' he said.
'We might pick up clothes.
I got a good coat off them last year.'
Reg nodded but Tom knew it would be
up to him to get stuff for them both.
Reg could not fend for himself.

So it was Tom who waited
for the STREET AID van.
Tom who fought his way to the front.
Tom who begged for something for his friend.
'Here,' he told Reg later.
'That's the best I could do.'
He handed him a worn out cardigan.
Reg looked at it sadly.
'There's a button missing,' he said.
'What did you get for yourself?'
Tom's eyes shone.

Reg had never seen him so happy.

He pulled open a plastic bag.

'I got these shoes,' he said.

Tom lay in his sleeping bag

in the shop doorway.

He hugged the shoes to his chest.

He ran his fingers over the smooth leather.

He felt the pattern made by the tiny holes

punched round the heel and toe.

The laces were as good as new.

The soles were hardly worn at all.

and they were the right size.

'Real leather,' Reg had said. 'Hand made.

They must have cost a packet.

You've done well Tom.'

He sounded cross.

Tom knew he was jealous.

He was sorry about the tatty cardigan

but the moment he saw the shoes

he could not think of anything else.

He had to have them.

He had pushed in front of old Ben,

to snatch them from the woman's hand.

They made him think of Jack who had once

lent him a pair just like these.

'They can't be the same ones,' he told himself.

'That was years ago. Back in war time.'

3

Jack

He had met Jack at an RAF camp
where they did their basic training.
'Square bashing,' they called it then.
At first he'd been put off by Jack's manner,
his posh voice.
He didn't look the sort to bother
with a lad from a pit village.
But Jack wasn't a snob.
All the blokes took to him.

He was full of life. He made them laugh.

Jack was always in trouble.
For being late back to camp,
for having dirty boots, or long hair.
But the officers often let him off.
Even the drill sergeant who gave them
such a hard time. They all liked Jack.
He had such a way with him.
Tom and Jack lived in the same hut.
Tom was to train for the ground crew,
as a mechanic, working on the planes.
Jack set his sights higher.
He wanted to be a pilot.
Even when he knew he'd been chosen
he never put on airs and graces.
Jack was still one of the lads.
He'd lend you his last penny
– or his best shoes.

Tom remembered the night
of the dance.
Everyone was going.
It was a big affair
with a top band from London.
On his way out Jack found Tom
sitting on his bed
still wearing his overalls.
'What's up, old chap?' he said.
'Not getting your glad rags on?'
Tom felt shy of telling Jack he had
no decent shoes to wear but Jack
soon found out what the trouble was.
'No problem,' he said, going to his locker.
He came back with a smart brown pair.
'You can borrow mine.'

After this the two young men became
the best of friends.

They spent all their free time together.

Tom began to dread the day

when they would part.

He was going to an air base

on the east coast.

Jack to flying school.

Tom told Jack how much he'd miss him.

'Don't worry,' Jack said.

'Keep in touch.

We'll meet up when the war's over.

And I'll be up there watching over you.'

In fact, Tom never saw him again.

He heard a few months later that Jack

had been killed in action.

He was just nineteen years old.

'How young we were,' Tom thought now

as he lay in his cold make-shift bed.

'What a long time ago it seems.'

4

New Life

After Tom got the shoes
things took a turn for the better.
The weather was warm and he felt fitter
than he had done for ages.
The shoes seemed to give him
a new lease of life.
It was just as if Jack was beside him
as in the old days, keeping him cheerful.
Reg didn't like the change in Tom.

'Slow down,' he'd grumble.

'What's the rush.'

He couldn't keep up with him.

Tom took to walking

further and further each day.

He began to move away from his old patch,

near the railway arches.

Once he walked along the river bank.

Another day he found a lovely park.

He never knew where he would finish up.

It was as if his feet had a will of their own.

One night he missed his supper.

'The van came ages ago,' Reg told him.

'They wouldn't let me have two pies.

I ate mine. I didn't know when you'd be back.'

Tom didn't say anything.

He thought of all the times he'd stood

in the queue and begged for food for Reg.

But then Reg wasn't really a true friend.
Not like Jack had been.

Besides, Tom knew something would turn up.
He wouldn't go to sleep hungry.
When he found a pound coin
in the gutter that night
he became more and more sure
that Jack was somehow looking after him.

5

Home At Last

One morning Tom woke from a strange dream

in which he saw Jack's face and

heard his voice. Jack had told him

they were to meet quite soon.

Tom got up and put his bundle together.

He hid it, as always, in the churchyard.

Then he set off, walking quickly.

He did not know where he was heading.

His feet seemed to take him

through the streets, away from the inner city,
into an area he did not know.

Suddenly, ahead of him he caught sight
of a figure he knew well.
Even though he only saw the back
of the young man's head he knew
at once that it was Jack.
'Wait,' he shouted.
'Hang on, Jack, it's me, Tom.'
But the other man did not slow down.
Tom almost ran through the streets
trying to catch up with him.
However fast he went Jack always
seemed to be the same distance away.

Soon Tom felt quite worn out.
His legs were tired, his feet ached.
His heart was banging away in his chest.

He badly wanted to slow down,

take a rest and get his breath back.

But he dared not stop.

Not when there was a chance he might

meet up with Jack once again.

The houses in this part of town were big.

They had nice front gardens with lawns,

stained glass panes in their front doors.

It was just the sort of area

where Jack might have lived.

Tom got excited.

He forgot that he was old and poor.

He forgot that Jack was long since dead.

He felt sure they would soon be together.

As he turned the next corner

he spotted Jack going into a house

at the end of the street.

Tom almost ran in his hurry to reach it.

His feet stopped in front of a large house,

set in its own grounds.

Feeling sure that this was the right one,

Tom went up the path and rang the bell.

There was no answer. He rang again.

Then he saw that the door had been left ajar,

as if to invite him in.

He went down the hall, calling softly.

There was no-one about.

At the end of the hall was a kitchen.

It was warm and cosy with a fire

burning in the grate. From the oven came

the smell of roasting meat.

Tom looked around.

It was not a modern room.

It was done up the way kitchens had been

when he was a boy.

Washing hung from a rack.

Blue and white china filled a dresser.

One place was set out ready at the table

on a snowy white cloth.

Tears came to Tom's eyes.

It was as if he had come home at last.

Inside the oven he found a meal keeping warm.

Tom sat in the armchair by the fire.

For the first time in years

his stomach felt really full.

He could not remember when he had last

eaten such a good meal.

Roast beef with Yorkshire pudding,

mashed potatoes, carrots and sprouts.

Then apple pie with thick creamy custard.

There had even been a glass of beer

to wash it all down.

He knew without a doubt that this

was Jack's doing.

That he would soon appear

to talk over old times.

Tom settled back in the armchair.

He took off his jacket and undid his shoes.

Slipping them off, he leaned back

in the warmth of the firelight to wait.

6

The Bomb Site

A postman found Tom's body
when he was out
on his early morning round.
It gave him a nasty shock as he told
his wife later, finding the old man
lying stiff and cold on the wasteground.
His shoes were lying next to him.
Reg read about his friend's death later
in a week-old newspaper.

Tom hadn't been harmed, the paper said.

There were no marks on his body.

He had simply died of cold,

falling asleep on a freezing night

out on the bomb site.

It was, said the paper,

one where a British plane

had crashed fifty years before, in fog,

coming back from a night raid over Germany.